STEM Superstars

Mae Jemison

by Rachel Castro

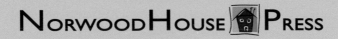

NORWOOD HOUSE PRESS

Cover: Jemison still studies space.

Norwood House Press
Chicago, Illinois

For information regarding Norwood House Press, please visit our website at:
www.norwoodhousepress.com or call 866-565-2900.

Hardcover ISBN: 978-1-68450-920-1
Paperback ISBN: 978-1-68404-460-3

Library of Congress Cataloging-in-Publication Data
Names: Castro, Rachel, author.
Title: Mae Jemison / by Rachel Castro.
Description: Chicago, Illinois : Norwood House Press, [2020] | Series: STEM superstars |
   Includes bibliographical references and index.
Identifiers: LCCN 2018061511 (print) | LCCN 2019002410 (ebook) | ISBN 9781684044658
   (ebook) | ISBN 9781684509201 (hardcover) | ISBN 9781684044603 (pbk.)
Subjects: LCSH: Jemison, Mae, 1956---Juvenile literature. | African American women
   astronauts--Biography--Juvenile literature. | Astronauts--United States--Biography--
   Juvenile literature. | African American women--Biography--Juvenile literature.
Classification: LCC TL789.85.J46 (ebook) | LCC TL789.85.J46 C37 2020 (print) | DDC
   629.45/0092 [B] --dc23
LC record available at https://lccn.loc.gov/2018061511

319N—072019
Manufactured in the United States of America in North Mankato, Minnesota

★ Table of Contents ★

Chapter 1

Early Life

Mae Jemison was born in 1956. Her family lived in Alabama. They moved to Chicago, Illinois, when she was three years old.

Jemison considers Chicago, Illinois, her home.

Experiments can be fun but should be done with an adult's help.

Jemison liked science. She ran **experiments**. Her parents gave her ideas. Her mom was a teacher. Her dad was a carpenter. They supported her love of science.

Jemison spent many hours in the library. She read about the stars. She learned about space.

As a child, Jemison liked learning about the stars.

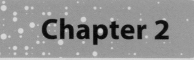

Chapter 2

School and Dance

Jemison liked dance. She took theater in high school. She was in her school government.

Jemison learned how to speak to groups when she was in school government.

Like these students, Jemison liked to dance.

Jemison studied **engineering** and African American studies. She took dance and theater classes in college, too.

Did You Know?
Jemison speaks
four languages.

Jemison then studied medicine. She became a doctor. She joined the **Peace Corps**. She worked in Sierra Leone and Liberia. These are two countries in western Africa. She was there for two years.

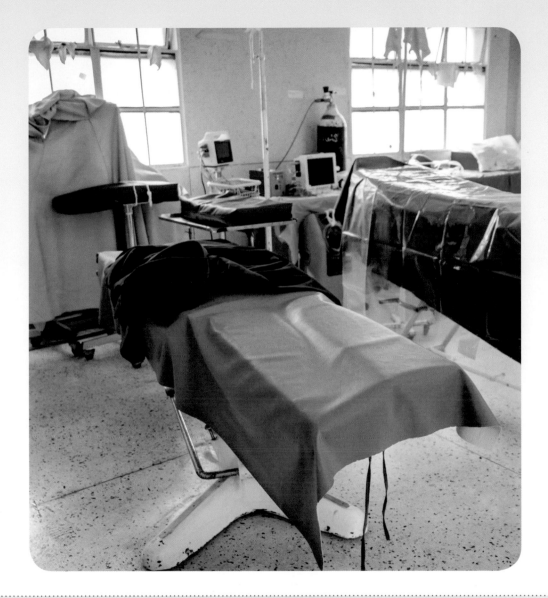

Jemison helped at hospitals in Africa.

Chapter 3

Going to Space

Jemison worked as a doctor. She was still curious about space. She applied to join **NASA**. She wanted to be an astronaut. NASA chose her. She trained for one year.

Jemison's training helped her get ready for space.

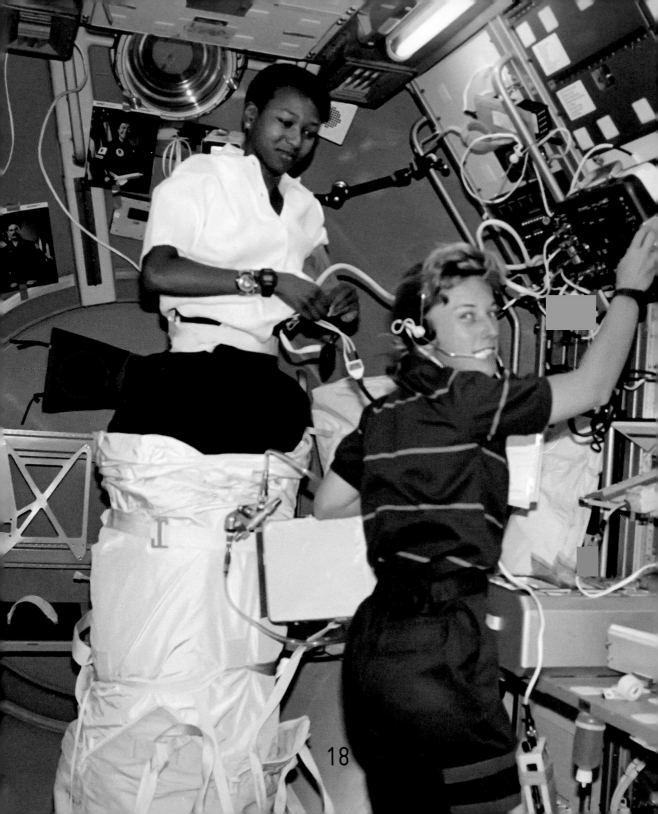

18

Jemison went on the space shuttle. She **orbited** Earth. She was the first African American woman in space. She ran medical tests on the astronauts.

Jemison did experiments on how space affects bones.

Did You Know?
Jemison has a high school in Alabama named after her.

Today, Jemison runs a technology company. She also encourages kids to study science. She still works on space projects.

Jemison still likes to learn about the stars.

★ Career Connections ★

1 Start by doing experiments at home, just like Jemison. With the help of an adult, you can use household items to conduct safe and simple experiments.

2 Check to see if a local library may have a STEM club, an astronomy program, or even STEM kits to check out. You can also ask a librarian to help you find books about science.

3 Jemison used to look up at the stars as a kid. You can do this in your backyard or at a park. Certain apps can help you find constellations, a space station, or specific stars.

4 If you're interested in medicine, ask a parent or guardian for an anatomy kit. It can help you learn about the human body and how it works.

5 Jemison started a science camp for kids six to twelve years old. It promotes science reading for students. Visit jemisonfoundation.org to learn more about how you can participate!

★ Glossary ★

engineering (en-juh-NIHR-ing): The science of designing and improving products or machines.

experiments (ek-SPER-uh-ments): Tests to try and discover something.

NASA (NASS-uh): National Aeronautics and Space Administration, an American agency that is responsible for air and space technology.

orbited (or-BIT-ed): Having followed the curved path that an object takes in space as it moves around a star, planet, or moon.

Peace Corps (PEESS KOR): A volunteer program that sends Americans to help with projects in developing countries.

★ For More Information ★

Books

Jennifer Strand. *Mae Jemison*. Minneapolis, MN: ABDO Zoom, 2017. Read this book to learn more about Mae Jemison.

Martha E. H. Rustad. *Becoming an Astronaut*. North Mankato, MN: Capstone Press, 2018. Read this book to learn about what it is like to be an astronaut.

Websites

The Biology Corner

(https://www.biologycorner.com/category/worksheets/anatomy/) This page has articles and activities to help teach kids about the human body.

NASA Kids' Club

(https://www.nasa.gov/kidsclub/index.html) On this page, kids can learn more about space and the space program.

⋆ Index ⋆

⋆ About the Author ⋆

Rachel Castro is a Minneapolis-based writer. She holds degrees in English literature and creative nonfiction. In addition to writing for the educational market, she works for a public library and teaches creative writing.